THE BEST BOOK OF Football Songs and Chants Ever!

THE BEST BOOK OF Football Songs and Chants Ever!

DAVID HULMES

CARLTON

Contents

Foreword
by Nick Hancock

Quite honestly, you can stuff your World Cup up your ... jumper. I've recently returned from France and my first live experience of the beautiful game's ultimate competition, and, if I'm truthful, I'm a little disappointed. Don't get me wrong, I saw some wonderful football, some beautiful cities, and some awesome stadia; but somehow, something was missing.

The truth of the matter is that, for all their flamboyance, skill, technical brilliance and penalty-taking abilities, countries from outside Britain and Ireland can't sing a football song to save their lives.

The Brazilians may have their Samba style, the Dutch their orange hats, the Iranians their unbridled passion, but when it comes to songs the rest of the world are The Smurfs to our Oasis. The England and Scotland games were on a different planet to the other games I saw and so, inevitably, the atmosphere was incomparable.

I sat through the Brazil versus Holland semi-final and can honestly say that the crowd had none of the wit, banter and inventiveness present at the average Stoke City versus Leek Town friendly.

Football songs are a central part of the game over here and we can be justifiably proud of the peculiar way in which they evolve. Some are a little cruel, some politically dubious and one or two are simply moronic – but many are genuinely witty and inspired. Indeed, for those of you, like me, who support one of football's less-fashionable clubs, their are times when the songs provide saturday afternoon's only meaningful entertainment!

Enjoy and then argue over which song is really whose!

Nick Hancock
August 1998

Introduction

I can't remember the first time I went to a football match, except to say it would have been in the early 1970s. Similarly, I'm sure I'm not the only football fan who finds it all too easy to forget what has happened in most matches I watch (4–3 thrillers excepted) within a day or two.

It's because most matches are so depressingly ordinary they fail to leave an impression. Of course, you can remember the score, the scorers, how the goals were scored and the other important bits, but most of it will have drifted into the wastebasket of our memories within a very short space of time. Not so the chants and songs. We've all got our favourites, but the ones which really stick in our minds can often come from an unlikely source – the opposing fans.

You know the kind of thing. Your side's playing rubbish, so badly that they can't see off the worst excuse of a football team that they've seen in years; it's blowing a gale and chucking it down; the half-time pies were rubbish and none of the players look capable of scoring in a brothel let alone on the pitch – and then, all of a sudden, the supporters of the other team belt out, 'We're shit and we're sick of it' (and it's only October).

Now not only does that give us all a bit of a laugh but here we have, in one simple line, a succinct and definitive expression of what those fans think of being treated to such a crap display when they've taken a half-day off to travel halfway across the country for the second leg of a cup competition that changes its name once a season.

And though we might have a good laugh at their expense, there is a serious side to all this vocal hilarity. Their frustration could be borne of terminally inept boardroom members, a manager who can't tell his Vauxhall Conference from his Rymans League or players desperately short on talent.

But what effect does the chanting have? Well, the players certainly hear it, as does the management and whichever board members have bothered to show up. Surely, it prompts some reaction in them. I hope so, because it's the fans who create the atmosphere and they have a right to respect from the clubs they support. If they stopped going, where would the game be?

In compiling this book I've tried to reflect the contemporary and the best of yesteryear while attempting to retain a sense of originality for each club. However, with all the best will in the world, some clubs' fans do lack imagination, and they tend to be the ones which also lack success. Some were able to supply only the flimsiest of offerings for this collection. Indeed, Bury told me they had no supporters' club and no fanzine which goes to confirm what we Bolton fans have known about them for years: Shit ground, no fans!

David Hulmes, London, August 1998

English football Clubs

ARSENAL

We've got that Double feeling
(To the tune of 'You've lost that loving feeling')

We've got that Double feeling
Oohh, that Double feeling
We've got that Double feeling
'Cos it's on, on, on...

Arsenal chant (1)

One nil to the Arsenal
(etc.)

Arsène Wenger's magic

Arsène Wenger's magic
He wears a magic hat
And when he saw the double
He said I'm having that
Ooooooo
(repeat)

Arsenal chant (2)

We'll win, 'cos we're Arsenal

Nicolas Anelka

La, la, la, la, la, la An-el-ka
La, la, la, la, la, la An-el-ka
La, la, la, la, la, la An-el-ka
LA, LA, LA, LA, LA, LA An-el-ka

Emmanuel Petit (pre-World Cup)

He's blond, he's quick
His name's a porno flick
Emmanuel, Emmanuel

Emmanuel Petit (post-World Cup)

He's quick, he's blond
He won the Coup du Monde
Emmanuel, Emmanuel

She wore a yellow ribbon

She wore, she wore, she wore a yellow ribbon
She wore a yellow ribbon
In the merry month of May
And when I asked her why she wore that ribbon
She said it's for the Arsenal
And we're going to Wem-ber-lee
Wem-ber-lee Wem-ber-lee
We're the famous Ar-se-nal
And we're going to Wem-ber-lee

Arsenal chant (3)

Boring, boring Arsenal!
*(Sung by the North Bank when Arsenal
are winning comprehensively)*

We've got a foreskin more than you
(To the tune of 'She'll be coming round the mountain')

We'll be running round Wembley with our
willies hanging out
We'll be running round Wembley with our
willies hanging out
We'll be running round Wembley
Running round Wembley
Running round Wembley with our
willies hanging out

Singing we've got a foreskin more than you
We've got a foreskin more than you
We've got a foreskin
We've got a foreskin
We've got a foreskin more than you

Sheringham chants

Oooooo, Teddy, Teddy
He went to Man United
And he won fuck all

You'll win fuck all again
Sheringham, Sheringham

One man and his dog

One man went to laugh, went to laugh at Chelsea
One man and his dog (Spot), went to laugh at Chelsea
(*repeat up to ten men*)

Patrick Vieira

He comes from Senegal
He plays for Arsenal
Vieira, o-o-o-o-oh Vieira (*etc.*)

Arsenal chant (4)

Hark now, hear the Arsenal sing
The Tottenham run away
And we will fight forever more
Because of Boxing Day

ASTON VILLA

Dwight Yorke
(To the tune of 'New York, New York')

Start spreading the news
He's playing today
I want to see him score again
Dwight Yorke, Dwight Yorke

If he can *(pause)* score from there
He'll score from *(pause)* anywhere
It's up to you
Dwight Yorke, Dwight Yorke
De de, dedede, de de dedede

(obviously not sung since 'Yorkie' left for Manchester United)

Roll along

Roll along, Aston Villa, roll along
To the top of the League where you belong
There'll be cups and trophies too
For the boys in Claret 'n' Blue
Roll along, Aston Villa, roll along

Sing when we're shopping

Sing when we're shopping, we only sing when
we're shopping
*(in the Normid End at Bolton's former home,
Burnden Park)*

A footballer called Dwight Yorke
(To the tune of 'An Englishman in New York')

When he's on the pitch at Villa Park
And he's really on his game
He can twist and turn and score a goal!
Everybody knows his name!

Ooooooooooo, he's a footballer
An Aston Villa footballer
He's a footballer called Dwight Yorke

Sign on

(To the tune of 'You'll Never Walk Alone',
when playing Liverpool)

Sign on, sign on
With a pen in your hand
'Cos you'll ne-ver work a-gain
You'll ne-ver work again
Sign on, sign on

Go once a season

Go once a season
You only go once a season
Go once a season
(to Man Utd and Liverpool)

BARNET

A nine-point Christmas
(To the tune of 'White Christmas')

I'm dreaming of a nine-point Christmas
Just like the ones I used to know
Where the goalposts glistened
And children listened
To hear the West Bank in full flow (in full flow)

Why don't you fuck off Alan Mullery
(To the tune of 'Don't Cry For Me Argentina')

Why don't you fuck off Alan Mullery
The truth is we never liked you
Now we are losing
Now we are shit
Why don't you fuck off
You sad fat git

The Fulham train

(To the tune of 'The Runaway Train')

The Fulham train came over the hill, hurrah, hurrah
The Fulham train came over the hill, hurrah, hurrah
The Fulham train came over the hill
The brakes failed and they all got killed
Lala la-la la-la
The brakes failed and they all got killed

Barnet chant

We all follow the Bar-net
Over land and sea (and Runcorn)
We'll all follow the Flash-man to the cemetery
('Land of Hope and Glory' version during the
1992–93 season when Stan Flashman led the club to the
brink of extinction)

My old man's a dustman

My old man's a dustman
He wears a fireman's hat
He killed 10,000 Germans
So what d'ya think of that
One lay here, one lay there, one lay round
the corner
A poor ol' soul with a bullet up his hole was
crying out for water
Water, water, water, water came at last
I don't want your water so stick it up your
As-k her round for tea, and all the family
If she don't come I'll tickle her bum with a lump
of celery
Celery, celery
If she don't come I'll tickle her bum with a lump
of celery

West Bank Underhill

Balls right, skin back tight
Bollocks to the front
We're the boys who make more noise and we're
always on for cunt
We're the riders of the night and we love to
fucking fight
We're the riders of the West Bank Underhill

BARNSLEY

Lars Lees

He aims (he's tall)
To please (as trees)
He takes the ball with ease
Lars Lees, Lars Lees

Barnsley chant

D-I-WAN-KEY-O
D-I-WAN-KEY-O
D-I-WAN-KEY-O
*(Tune of 'D-I-S-C-O', aimed at Sheffield Wednesday's
Paulo Di Canio)*

Brazil

Bra-zil
It's just like watching Brazil
It's just like watching Brazil
It's just like watching Brazil
Bra-zil
*(Popular during 1996–97 promotion season,
but no reason to sing it since)*

BIRMINGHAM CITY

Shit on the Villa

Shit on the Villa
Shit on the Villa tonight

Birmingham chant
(To the tune of 'Oh When the Saints')

My garden shed
Is bigger than this
My garden shed
Is bigger than this
It's got a door
And a window
My garden shed
Is bigger than this.
*(Sung by City fans when visiting some of the
smaller grounds in the League)*

Don't cry for me Aston Villa

Don't cry for me Aston Villa
The truth is I cannot stand you
All through my wild days
My mad existence
We took the Holte End
Without resistance

Birmingham City FC

And it's Birmingham City
Birmingham City FC
We're by far the greatest team
The world has ever seen

BLACKPOOL

We hate Preston North End

When I was a young boy
I asked my father what would I be
Should I be Blackpool or PNE
This is what he said to me:
Wash your mouth out son
And get your father's gun
And shoot some Preston scum,
shoot some Preston scum

Ooooooooo, we hate Preston North End,
We hate Preston too
And Preston
We hate Preston North End and
Preston weeeee hate you

Cheer up Stan Ternent
(To the tune of 'Daydream Believer')

Cheer up Stan Ternent
O what can it be
For those
Sad Burnley bastards
And a
Shit football team

Blackpool chant

Chim, chiminee, chim, chiminee
Chim, chim, cherou
We hate the bastards in claret and blue
(Burnley by any chance?)

BOLTON WANDERERS

Bolton chant (1)

Can we play you every week?
*(Credited with being the first to sing this during the 4–1 win
at Middlesbrough in February 1996, when rooted to
the foot of the Premier League)*

Bolton chant (2)

Where were you when you were shit?
*(to Blackburn's new-found jump-on-the-
Jack-Walker-bandwagon fans)*

Bolton chant (3)

Fiiiiiiiiiish
*(Adopted South African chant for whenever
Mark Fish touches the ball)*

Bolton barmy army

Oooooooooooooooooohhhhhhhhhhhh
We keep chickens (Feeeesh) in our back yard (tank)
We feed 'em ('im) on Indian (African) corn
And one's a bugger for giving the other
A piggy back over the wall
O we're the barmy Bolton army na-na-na-na-na
na na
ner ner

Mixu Paateleinen

(To the tune of 'There's No Limit')

Mixu
Mixu Mixu
Mixu Mixu
Mixu Paaa-te-leinen

Run, run wherever you may be

Run, run wherever you may be
We are the BWFC
And we'll twat you up
Wherever you may be
And put you in the infirmary

John McGinlay

We've got something you've not got
We've got something you've not got
We've got something you've not got
Super John McGinlay
Super, super John
Super, super John
Super, super John
Super John McGinlay

I was born under a Wanderers scarf

(To the tune of 'I was born under a Wandering Star')

I was born
Under a Wanderers scarf
I was born
Under a Wanderers scarf
Knives are made for stabbing
Guns are made to shoot
If you come in the Lever End we'll all stick in
the boot
I was born under a Wanderers scarf

Bolton chant (4)

What the fuck
What the fuck
What the fuck is going on?
*(Scarborough's first-ever Football League victory, a 4–0 thrashing
of Bolton in 1987, is greeted with understandable incredulity)*

BOURNEMOUTH

Fratton Park is falling down
(To the tune of 'London Bridge is Falling Down')

Fratton Park is falling down
Falling down, falling down
Fratton Park is falling down
Poor old Pompey

Build it up with red and black
Red and black
Red and black
Build it up with red and black
Poor old Pompey

Play up Boscombe Town

Play up Boscombe Town
Never let us down
Score a goal and score some more
You're the team that we adore
Win the game today
Win them all away
Play up Boscombe
Play up Boscombe
Play up Boscombe Town
(Club was known as Bournemouth
& Boscombe AFC until 1972)

Bournemouth chant

I've travelled this land for many a year
Spent all my money on football and beer
Supporting the Bournemouth is why we are here
And we'll get promotion in less than a year

We are the Bournemouth

We are the Bournemouth
We play at Dean Court
We live beside the seaside, but we haven't got a port
Pompey have got one, Scum have one as well
Pompey play at Fratton Park and Scummers
fucking smell

Stevie Fletcher

Stevie, Stevie, Stevie, Stevie Fletcher
Score another goal for me
Stevie, Stevie, Stevie, Stevie Fletcher
It's nearly half past three
We haven't had a goal for half-an-hour and it's nearly
time for tea
So Stevie, Stevie, Stevie, Stevie Fletcher
Score another goal for me

BRADFORD CITY

Bradford chant (1)

Come on you yellows
*(Unoriginal but, even worse, City actually play
in claret and amber shirts, not yellow)*

Dino

Dino, Dino, Dino
(Brazilian star Edinho is the inspiration for this one)

Bradford chant (2)

(Clapping to the rhythm of...)
1–2
1–2–3
1–2–3–4
City!

BRIGHTON & HOVE ALBION

Brighton chant (1)

They've sold the ground
And now we're going down
Sack the board, sack the board

Build a bonfire, build a bonfire
Put Bell-otti on the top
Put Bill Archer in the middle
And burn the fucking lot

*(Chief Executive David Bellotti and Chairman Archer bear the
brunt of protests during the south coast club's crisis)*

Brighton chant (2)

In 1983 we went to Wembley
To play Man United and make history
Robbo was through, but he passed it to Smith
The stupid Scotch bastard was pissed and he missed

And it's Brighton Hove Albion
Brighton Hove Albion FC
We're by far the greatest team
The world has ever seen

Stick your fucking Priestfield up yer arse

You can stick your fucking Priestfield up yer arse
You can stick your fucking Priestfield up yer arse
You can stick your fucking Priestfield
Stick your fucking Priestfield
Stick your fucking Priestfield up yer arse
(Gillingham's stadium proves far from a
home from home for the exiles)

Brighton chant (4)

P-A-L-A-C-E
Stevie Coppell's got VD
With a nick nack paddy whack
Give the dog a bone
Crystal Palace fuck off home

Brighton chant (5)

Come with me and have a cup of tea in
Stevie Coppell's garden
Jump on his head until the fucker's dead
In Stevie Coppell's garden
*(Former Palace manager Coppell cops the brunt of Brighton's
intense hatred of all things to do with the south London club)*

Brighton chant (6)

If you're all going to Mellor clap your hands
*(The fans seem quite keen on a pilgrimage
to Bill Archer's home village)*

BRISTOL ROVERS

Irene, Goodnight Irene

We're loyal supporters, we're faithful and true
We always follow, the boys in blue (and white)
We all made a promise, that we'll never part
So Goodnight Irene, I'll see you in my dreams

('Irene, Goodnight Irene' was regularly played at Rovers'
former home Eastville from the 1950s. The bit that goes:
'Sometimes I have a great notion, to jump in the river and
drown,' would have appealed to fans after watching their team
lose, as the river ran alongside the ground)

Who's that team

Who's that team they call the City
Who's that team that never scores
And they play in red and white
And they're a load of shite
And their manager's mother is a whore

We're Gas

We're Gas and we're going up
We're Gas and we're going up
We're Gas and we're going up
*(Eastville was next to a gas works. Fans said that
when the heads of the gasometers were rising, the smell
overcame the opposition and helped Rovers win,
hence the name Gasheads)*

You've got me singing the Blues!

I never felt more like singing the Blues
Than when Rovers win, and City lose
Oooo Rovers
You've got me singing the Blues!
We hate Joe Jordan, and all of the reds
The only good City fan is one that's dead
Oooo Rovers
You've got me singing the Blues!

Red, red Robin

When the red, red, robin goes bob, bob
bobbin' along
Shoot the bastard
Shoot the bastard
Shoot, shoot, shoot the bastard

He's only a poor little robin

He's only a poor little Robin
His wings are all tattered and torn
He made me feel sick
So I hit him with a brick
And now he don't sing any more!

Number four is a horse's arse

Number four, number four, number four is a
horse's arse
He's the meanest
He sucks a horse's penis
Number four is a horse's arse
He looks like a horse's arse!
He smells like a horse's arse!
He IS a horse's arse!
(Doesn't have to be number four, obviously!)

You're shit

Oooooooooooooor!
You're shit ahhhhhhh!
You've got AIDS ahhhhhhh
You suck cocks ahhhhhhhh
You shag sheep ahhhhhhhhhhhhh!
(One for the visiting 'keeper)

Aston Gate is full of shit

Oh Ashton Gate (oh Ashton Gate)
Is full of shit (is full of shit)
Oh Ashton Gate is full of shit
Full of shit, shit and more shit
Oh Ashton Gate is full of shit

BURNLEY

One man and his dog

One man went to shit
Went to shit on Ewood
One man and his dog (Spot)
Went to shit on Ewood

Two men went to shit
Went to shit on Ewood
Two men and their dog (Spot)
Went to shit on Ewood

(Repeat up to ten)

He's fucked off home

He's fucked off home
He's fucked off home
He's fucked off
Shearer's fucked off home
(After the striker quit Blackburn for Newcastle)

Burnley chant

Why are your pies so shit?
(Sung at Swansea City in the early 1980s)

CAMBRIDGE UNITED

Cheer up Barry Fry
(To the tune of 'Daydream Believer')

Cheer up Barry Fry
Oh what can it mean
To a fat 'Boro bastard
And a shit football team

Billy Beall

Billy Beall, Billy Beall
Billy Billy Beall
He gets the ball and scores a goal
Billy Billy Beall

Cambridge chant

1–2 (clap, clap)
1–2–3 (clap,clap,clap)
1–2–3–4 (clap,clap,clap,clap)
5–1 (clap,clap)
(Reference to an ancient 5–1 win at Peterborough)

CARDIFF CITY

Do the Ayatollah

(Fans crouch and rise slowly)
oooooooooooOOOOOO!
(Fans start slapping their foreheads)
Do the Ayatollah
Do the Ayatollah
Nerner ner ner
Nerner ner ner
(This bizarre offering of a few years ago is explained by television footage from Iran when news of the Ayatollah Khomeini's death spread. People took to the streets slapping their heads as a sign of grief and, as the Bluebirds were having a bad time of things themselves around then, they adopted this chant as a symbol of grief at their predicament)

It's full of shit

It's full of shit, it's full of shit
It's full of…
England's full of shit

Cardiff chant

1–0 to the sheep shaggers

You Jack bastard

You Jack bastard, you Jack bastard

(Misheard by some national newspaper reporters as 'You black bastard' at an FA Cup tie with Reading in February 1998. The chant was directed at one of Reading's players, once of Swansea City. The Jack bit refers to the Swansea Jack, a pub just outside the Vetch Field and the chant is reserved for Swansea fans or ex-Swansea players)

CARLISLE UNITED

We're going up

We're going up, we're going up
We're going, Carlisle's going up

If you're proud

If you're proud to be a Cumbrian clap your hands!

We'd rather shag a sheep

We'd rather shag a sheep than a Mackem
We'd rather shag a sheep than a Mackem
Oh we'd rather shag a sheep
Rather shag a sheep
Rather shag a sheep than a Mackem

Carlisle chant
(Can Can tune with lots of high kicking)

1–0 to the sheep shaggers

We are Carlisle

We are Carlisle, super Carlisle, we are Carlisle,
from the north
No one likes us, no one likes us, but we are Carlisle
and we don't care
'Cos we are Carlisle, super Carlisle, we are Carlisle,
from the north

We are Cumbrians

Cumbrians, we are Cumbrians
Cumbrians, we are Cumbrians
Cumbrians, we are Cumbrians
Oh yes, we are Cumbrians

CHARLTON ATHLETIC

Stand up ... sit down

Stand up, if you hate Millwall
Sit down, if you hate Palace

Mark Kinsella
(To the tune of 'Do the Macarena')

Oooooo Mark Kinsella

Valley Floyd Road
(To the tune of 'Mull of Kintyre')

Valley Floyd Road
Oh mist rolling in from the Thames
My desire is always to be here
Oh Valley Floyd Road

CHELSEA

One man went to mow

One man went to mow
Went to mow a meadow
One man and his dog (Spot)
Went to mow a meadow

Two men went to mow
Went to mow a meadow
Two men and their dog (Spot)
Went to mow a meadow

(Repeat up to ten men...)

The Blue Flag

Forever and ever we'll follow our team
For we are the Chelsea and we are supreme
We'll never be mastered by no northern bastards
And we'll keep the Blue Flag flying high
Flying high, up in the sky
We'll keep the Blue Flag flying high
From Stamford Bridge to Wemb(er)ley
We'll keep the Blue Flag flying high

When it's snowing

Sing when it's snowing
You only sing when it's snowing
Sing when it's snowing
*(Home leg of the 1997–98 European Cup-Winners' Cup tie
with Tromso of Norway, following a first leg played
during a snowstorm)*

Who's that team they call the Chelsea?

Who's that team they call the Chelsea?
Who's that team we all adore?
We're the boys in blue and white
And we fight with all our might
And we're out to show the world the way to score

Bring on Tottenham or the Arsenal
Bring on Scousers by the score
Barcelona, Real Madrid, Tottenham are a load of shits
And we're out to show the world the way to score

We all fucking hate Leeds

Leeds, Leeds and Leeds and Leeds
And Leeds
Leeds, and Leeds and Leeds
And Leeds, and Leeds and Leeds and Leeds
We all fucking hate Leeds

We are the famous CFC

Carefree wherever you may be
We are the famous CFC
And we don't give a fuck whoever you may be
'Cos we are the famous CFC

Frank Leboeuf (1)

He's here, he's there
He's every fucking where
Frank Leboeuf, Frank Leboeuf

Frank Leboeuf (2)

He's here, he's there
We're not allowed to swear
Frank Leboeuf, Frank Leboeuf
(Following a request from the player)

Vialli

He came from Italy
To play for Che-el-sea
Vialli, o-o-o-o-oh Vialli

CHESTER CITY

And we were killing the Wrexham bastards
(To the tune of 'And We Were Singing Hymns and Arias')

And we were killing the Wrexham bastards
In the land of their fathers
That's where'll they die

Chester Chant

Can you hear the Wrexham sing?
No-oh, no-oh
Can you hear the Wrexham sing?
No-oh, no-oh
Can you hear the Wrexham sing?
I can't hear a fucking thing
No-oh, no-oh no-oh

Those were the days

If you were born in Wales
You've probably heard the tales
Of Chester fans and what we do to you
We go to Wrexham town
And burn the stand right down
And build it up in royal blue and white
Die! Die! Die! Die Wrexham!

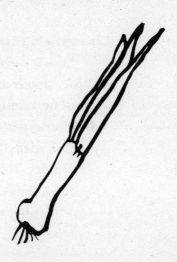

CHESTERFIELD

Burn the lot

Build a bonfire, build a bonfire
Put United on the top
Put the Wednesday in the middle
And burn the fucking lot
(A little ditty dedicated to the neighbouring Sheffield clubs)

Chesterfield chant

Skies are blue, clouds are white
God must be a Spireite
Derderderder
Derderder
Derder

Chim, chiminee

Chim, chiminee, chim, chiminee
Chim, chim, cherou
We hate the scabbing bastards
In yellow and blue
(To Mansfield in memory of the miners' strike)

Elleray

Elleray, Elleray,
We're the famous Chesterfield
And we were robbed by Elleray
*(After 1996–97 run to FA Cup semi-finals
was halted by the aforementioned referee)*

COVENTRY CITY

Go for it, City

Go for it
Go for it City
Sky Blues shooting to win

Mickey Quinn

He's fat, he's round
He scores on every ground
Mickey Quinn, Mickey Quinn

Shit on the Villa

Shit on the Villa
Shit on the Villa tonight

CREWE ALEXANDRA

Blue Moon

(Crewe are generally credited with being the first fans to sing this, and they sing it in its entirety, though it has since been adopted by Man City)

Ing-er-land

Ing-er-land, Ing-er-land, Ing-er-land
(reserved for Wrexham)

Crewe Chant

And its Crewe Alexandra
Crewe Alexandra FC
They're by far the greatest team
The world has ever seen

The Clayhead scum

When I was just a little boy, I asked my mother
what will it be
Will it be Vale? Will it be Stoke? Here's what
she said to me
Wash your mouth out son, and get your father's gun
And shoot the Clayhead scum
And shoot the Clayhead scum

Sheep shaggers

Sheep, sheep, sheep shaggers
(also reserved for Wrexham)

CRYSTAL PALACE

Eagles

Eagles, eagles, eagles

We are Palace

We are Palace, super Palace
We are Palace from Selhurst

Glad all over

Glad all over
*(The Dave Clark Five number one hit of 1964 is sung as the
teams run out at the start of the match)*

DARLINGTON

Sack the board

Sack the board, sack the board, sack the board
(Something the new owners will hope not to hear)

You're so crap

You're so crap you're worse than Hartlepool

I'm Henry the VIII

I'm Henry the VIII I am
I got married to the widow next door
She's been married seven times before
And everyone was a Henry
Never a Willy or a Sam

EVERTON

Ever-ton

Ever-ton, Ever-ton, Ever-ton
Ever-ton, Ever-ton, Ever-toonnnn
Ever-ton, Ever-ton, Ever-ton
Ever-ton, EVER-TON

You are my Everton

You are my Everton, my only Everton
You make me happy when skies are grey
You'll never know just how much I love you
So please never take my Everton away

It's a grand old team to play for

It's a grand old team to play for
It's a grand old team to support
And if you know the history
It's enough to make your heart go
Ooooooooooo

We don't care what the Red shite say
What the fuck do we care
We only know there's going to be a show
And the Everton boys will be there

EXETER CITY

We'll score again
(To the tune of 'We'll meet again')

We'll score again
Don't know where
Don't know when
But I know we'll score again some sunny day

Keep smiling through
Just like we always do
'Cos you know we'll score again
Some sunny day

Will you please say hello
To the folks that I know
And tell them I won't be long
You'll be happy to know
While we wait for a goal
We'll keep singing this song

We'll score again
Don't know where
Don't know when
But I know we'll score again some sunny day

Green and white cop
(To the tune of 'Yellow Submarine')

We all piss in a green and white kop
In a green and white kop
A green and white kop
A green and white kop

I comes from the West Country

I can't read and I can't write
But that don't really matter
'Cos I comes from the West Country
And I can drive a tractor

FULHAM

Can't live

I Can't live
If livin' is without you
*(The 1970s live on at Craven Cottage as this old hit is
sung on a regular basis)*

Dicks out

Dicks out
*(Under-fire boss Alan Dicks is called on to make the
ultimate sacrifice during the early part of the 90s)*

Sex case

Sex case, sex case, sex case
Hang him, hang him, hang him

Came for the ball boys

Came for the ball boys
You only came for the ball boys
*(These two are chanted at a particularly suspicious
looking member of the away support)*

You'll never play us...

You'll never play us again
*(When Brentford were heading for the basement division and it
seemed as if Fulham might be going up in the 1997–98 season)*

HARTLEPOOL UNITED

Hark now hear

Hark now hear, the 'Pool sing
The Darlo ran away
Where were you on Boxing Day?
The fighting started, you ran away

HUDDERSFIELD TOWN

Smile a while

There's a team that's dear to it's followers
Their colours are bright blue and white
They're a team of reknown, they're the talk
of the town
And the game of football is their delight

All the while upon the field of play
Thousands gladly cheered them on their way
Often you could hear them say
'Who can beat the Town today?'

Then the bells shall ring so merrily
Every goal shall be a memory
So town play up and bring the Cup
Back to Huddersfield

Those were the days

Those were the days my friend
I thought they'd never end
We won the League three times in a row
We won the FA Cup
And now we're going up
We are the Town
Oh yes, we are the Town

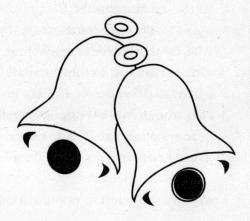

HULL CITY

Common Dolan

(To the tune of 'Common People' by Pulp)

He came from Rochdale with a lack of knowledge
He studied management at Bradford College
That's where I *(pause)*, caught his eye
He told me that he was a manager
I said: 'In that case you'd better come and
manage us'
He said: 'Fine'
And then, in three seasons' time
He said: 'I want to take you to the Vauxhall Conference
I want to do whatever Halifax do
I want to sign lots of crap old players
I want to watch this club slide out of view
And hoof, and hoof and hoof
Because
There's nothing left to dooooooooooo'

A black and amber team

(To the tune of 'Yellow Submarine')

In the town, where I was born
There's a teeeeeeaaaaaaaam
Called Hull City
And we make, the pilgrimage
On a Saturday, to Boothferry
We all follow a black and amber team
A black and amber team
Who sometimes play in green

Fuck off Terry Dolan
(To the tune of 'Daydream Believer')

Fuck off Terry Dolan
You took us to Division Three
You're a shit football manager
And so is Jeff Leeeeeeeeee

Bri McGinty

Och aye, super Bri
Och aye, super Bri
Och aye, super Bri
Super Bri McGinty!

My old man...

My old man said be a rugby fan
I said, 'Fuck off bollocks you're a cunt'

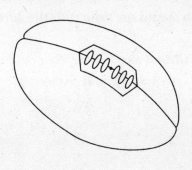

IPSWICH TOWN

The Blues

I never felt more like singing the Blues
When Ipswich win and Norwich lose
Oh Ipswich, you got me singing the Blues

I never felt more like singing the Blues
When Ipswich hit five, that's all right
Oh Ipswich, you got me singing the Blues

The moon and stars always shine
The super blues are fine, fine, fine
There's nothing else I'd rather do
Then spend my time with the super blues

*(Repeat second verse, then third verse
and finally first verse)*

He's only a poor little budgie

He's only a poor little budgie
His shirt is all tattered and torn
He started to sing
So we filled the cunt in
And now he don't sing anymore

The pride of Anglia

Who are the shits of Anglia?
Narrrrwich, Narrrrwich
Who are the pride of Anglia?
Ipswich, Ipswich
We're the pride of Anglia
Ipswich is our name

LEEDS UNITED

Marching on together

Here we go with Leeds United, we're going to give the
boys a hand
Stand up and sing for Leeds United, they're the
greatest in the land

Everyday we're all going to say we love you
Leeds, Leeds, Leeds
Everywhere we're all going to be there, we love you
Leeds, Leeds, Leeds
Marrrrrrr-ching on, together
We're gonna see you win
'Cos we're so proud
We shout it out loud
We love you Leeds, Leeds, Leeds

When I was just

When I was just a little boy
I asked my mother 'What should I be?'
'Should I be Chelsea?
Should I be Leeds?'
Here's what she said to me:
'Wash your mouth out son
And go get your father's gun
And shoot the Chelsea scum
Shoot the Chelsea scum'
(We hate Chelsea, we hate Chelsea)

We had joy

We had joy, we had fun
We had Man U on the run
But the joy didn't last
'Cos the bastards ran too fast!

Hark now hear

Hark now hear, United sing
The Man U ran away
And there will be a massacre
Upon this Saturday

Who do you think you are kidding Mr Ferguson
(The Dad's Army *theme tune)*

Who do you think you are kidding Mr Ferguson
If you think you'll win the League
We are the boys who will stop your little game
We are the boys who will win the League again

We are Leeds

We are Leeds, we are Leeds
We are Leeds
We are Leeds, we are Leeds
We are Lee-eeds
We are Leeds, we are Leeds
We are Leeds
We are Lee-eeds
We are Leeds!

LEICESTER CITY

Are you watching?

Are you watching
Are you watching
Are you watching Mark McGhee

Start the wave

Martin, start the wave
Martin, Martin start the wave

LINCOLN CITY

Shit refs

Shit refs and we're sick of 'em
(After a run of games poorly refereed at start of 1997–98 season)

We smell fish

We smell fish, we smell fish
(Turning noses up at rivals Grimsby Town)

Grant Brown

Ooooof, Grant Brown
Ooooof, Grant Brown
Ooooof, Grant Brown
(Celebrating another slice into the crowd)

LIVERPOOL

The reds are coming up the hill

The reds are coming up the hill, boys
The reds are coming up the hill, boys
They all laugh at us, they all laugh at us
They all say our days are numbered
Born to be a Scouse
Victorious are we
If you wanna win the Cup, then you'd better hurry up
'Cos Liverpool FC ...
Glorious, victorious ... *etc* ...

We all live in a red and white Kop

(To the tune of 'Yellow Submarine')

We all live in a red and white Kop
A red and white Kop
A red and white Kop
We all live in a red and white Kop
A red and white Kop
A red and white Kop
(Repeat forever)

Red river valley

Let me tell you the story of a poor boy
Who was sent far away from his home
To fight for his king and his country
And all the old folks back home
They put him in a second division
Sent him off to a far foreign field
Where the flies swarm around in their thousands
And there's nothing to see but the sand
Now the battle it started next morning
Under the Arabian sun
I remember the poor Scouser Tommy
Who was shot by an old Nazi gun
He lay on the battlefield dying
With the blood rushing out of his head
As he lay on the battlefield dying, dying, dying
These were the last words he said
'Oh, I'm a Liverpudlian and I come from the Spion Kop
I like to sing, I like to shout and get thrown out quite a
lot (every week)
We support a team that's dressed in red
It's a team that you all know
It's a team we call Li-ver-pool
And to glory we will go'

We won the League

We won the League, we won the League Cup
And we've been to Europe, too
We played the Toffees for a laugh
And left them feeling blue
1–0, 2–0, 3–0, 4–0, 5–0

On a Saturday afternoon

On a Saturday afternoon
We support a team called Liverpool
And we sing until we drop
On the famous Spion Kop

You'll Never Walk Alone

You'll Never Walk Alone
*(Anfield anthem, adopted by almost all other
clubs for at least a short while in the recent past)*

MANCHESTER CITY

What we love best

We fought in France, we fought in Spain
Fought in sun, we've fought in rain
We've taken the Kop, we've taken the Shed
But what we love best is kicking in Reds

Are you watching?

Are you watching?
Are you watching?
Are you watching Macclesfield
*(Final day relegation in 1997–98 season, despite a 5–2 victory
at Stoke City, was greeted with this ironic look forward to life in
the Second Division and future 'derby' meetings with their new
Cheshire-based rivals instead of short hops to Old Trafford)*

We never win

We never win at home and we never win away
We lost last week and we're losing today
We don't give a fuck
'Cos we're all pissed up
MCFC OK

Niall Quinn's disco pants

Niall Quinn's disco pants are the best
They come up from his arse to his chest
They're better than Adam and the Ants
Niall Quinn's disco pants
(Adopted after the former City striker
was seen out on the town one night)

Wonderwall

(To the tune of Oasis's 'Wonderwall')

And all the runs that Kinky makes are winding
And all the goals that City score are blinding
There are many times that we would like to score again
But we don't know how
'Cos maybe
You're gonna be the one that saves me
And after all
You're my Alan Ball

We've lost that Terry Phelan

(To the tune of 'We've Lost That Lovin' Feelin')

We've lost that Terry Phelan

We're not really here

We're not really here, we're not really here
Like the friends of the Invisible Man
We're not really here
(Inspired by City fans on tour in Ireland who trashed the bar of
the Metropole Hotel in Cork, then sung this to the police officers
sent to deal with the situation in the belief there was no proof
as to which ones were responsible)

Edghill

Edghill for England
(Defender comes in for ironic support as
City trail 6–0 at Liverpool)

City chant (1)

Oh Man City
The only English team to win the championship
(They claim no other team has won the
League title with 11 Englishmen)

City chant (2)

Oh Man City
The only football team to come from Manchester
(A dig at United's countrywide support)

City

In 1963 when we fell to Division Two
The Stretford End cried out aloud
'It's the end for you Sky Blue'
Joe Mercer came
We played the game
We went to Rotherham
And won 1–0
And we were back into Division One
We've won the League, we've won the League Cup
We've been to Europe too
And when we win the League again
We'll sing this song to you
City, City, City, City, City

MANCHESTER UNITED

Keano's magic

Oh, Keano's fucking magic
He wears a magic hat
And when he saw Old Trafford
He said, 'I fancy that'
He didn't sign for Arsenal
Or Blackburn 'cos they're shite
He signed for Man United
'Cos they're fucking dynamite

You are my Solskjaer
(To the tune of 'You are my Sunshine')

You are my Solskjaer
My Ole Solskjaer
You make me happy
When skies are grey
And Alan Shearer
Was fucking dearer
So please don't take
My Solskjaer, away

Paul Scholes

(To the tune of 'Kumbayah')

He scores goals m'lord, he scores goals
He scores goals m'lord, he scores goals
He scores goals m'lord, he scores goals
Paul Scholes, he scores goals

Ryan Giggs

Ryan Giggs, Ryan Giggs
Running down the wing
Ryan Giggs, Ryan Giggs
Running down the wing
Feared by the Blues
Loved by the Reds
Ryan Giggs, Ryan Giggs, Ryan Giggs

Drink, drink

(To the tune of 'Lord of the Dance')

Drink, drink wherever you may be
We are the drunk and disorderly
And we don't give a shit, and we don't give a fuck
We're going home with the European Cup!

Poor little Scouser

He's only a poor little Scouser
His face is all battered and torn
He made me feel sick
So I hit him with a brick
And now he don't sing anymore

I-yi yippie!

Singing i-yi yippie yippie-i
Singing i-yi yippie yippie-i
Singing i-yi yippie, i-yi yippie
I-yi yippie yippie-i
If you all hate Scousers clap your hands
If you all hate Scousers clap your hands
If you all hate Scousers, all hate Scousers
All hate Scousers clap your hands

In your Liverpool slums

In your Liverpool slums
In your Liverpool slums
You look in the dustbin for something to eat
You find a dead rat and you think it's a treat
In your Liverpool slums

In your Liverpool slums
In your Liverpool slums
You shit on the carpet, you piss in the bath
You finger your grandma, and think it's a laugh
In your Liverpool slums

In your Liverpool slums
In your Liverpool slums
You speak in an accent exceedingly rare
You wear a pink tracksuit and have curly hair
In your Liverpool slums

In your Liverpool slums
In your Liverpool slums
Your mum's on the game and your dad's in the nick
You can't get a job 'cos you're too fucking thick
In your Liverpool slums

We're the best behaved supporters in the land

We're the best behaved supporters in the land
We're the best behaved supporters in the land
We're the best behaved supporters
Best behaved supporters
Best behaved supporters in the land (when we win!)

We're a right bunch of bastards when we lose
We're a right bunch of bastards when we lose
We're a right bunch of bastards
Right bunch of bastards
Right bunch of bastards when we lose

If I had the wings of a sparrow

If I had the wings of a sparrow
If I had the arse of a crow
I'd fly over Maine Road tomorrow
And shit on the bastards below, below
Shit on, shit on
Shit on the bastards below, below
Shit on, shit on
Shit on the bastards below

One song

One song
You've only got one song
You've only got one song
(Directed at Leeds United)

MIDDLESBROUGH

Cock of the North

We are the 'Boro, the Cock of the North
We all hate Newcastle, and Sunderland of course
We all drink whisky and Newcastle Brown
The 'Boro boys are in town
Na na na … we are the 'Boro

We shall overcome

We shall overcome some day
Deep in my heart I do believe
We shall overcome some day

We are the 'Boro boys

'Ello, 'ello, we are the 'Boro boys
'Ello, 'ello, we are the 'Boro boys
We're the Ayresome Angels and we never miss a match
We all follow the 'Boro
*(A survivor despite the move from
Ayresome Park to the Riverside stadium)*

Who's that team

All the Geordies went to Rome to see the Pope
All the Geordies went to Rome to see the Pope
And this is what he said:
'Who's that team they call the 'Boro?
Who's that team we all adore?
Oh we play in red and white
And we're fucking dynamite
And we'll support the 'Boro ever more'

The Gianluca Festa chant

(*Fans chant the theme tune to cult television series* The Addams
Family, *with clapping rather than finger clicking, which goes
something like this*)

der-der der-der der-der
der-der der-der der-der
der-der der-der der-der
der-der der-der der
derderderder
(*clap clap*)
derderderder
(*clap, clap*)
derderderder
derdererder

MILLWALL

No one likes us

No one likes us,
No one likes us
No one likes us
We don't care
We are Millwall
Super Millwall
We are Millwall
From The Den

Millwall chant

Let 'em come, let 'em come let 'em come
Let 'em all come down to The Den
Let 'em come, let 'em come, let 'em come
We'll only have to beat them again
It's the best team in London
The best team of all
Everybody knows us
We are called Millwall

You Scots cunt

You Scots cunt
(To any Scottish player on the pitch)

NEWCASTLE UNITED

A Monkey's head

(To the tune of 'Yellow Submarine')

In the land, where I was born
Lives a man, with a monkey's head
And he went, to Sunderland
And his name, is Peter Reid
Altogether now
Peter Reid's got a fuckin' monkey's head
A fuckin' monkey's head
A fuckin' monkey's head
Peter Reid's got a fuckin' monkey's head
A fuckin' monkey's head
A fuckin' monkey's head

Drink, drink

Drink, drink, wherever we may be
We are the drunk and disorderly
And we will drink wherever we may be
For we are the drunk and disorderly

I was drunk last night
I was drunk the night before
And I'm gonna get drunk like I've never been drunk
before
'Cos when we're drunk we're as happy as can be
For we are the drunk and disorderly

When I go a-wandering
Along the cliffs of Dover
If I see a mackem cunt
I'll push the bastard over

We drink Ex
We drink Brown
We're gonna wreck your fuckin' town
Na na na naaaa
Na na naaaaa
Na naaaaa

Philippe Albert
(To the tune of 'Rupert the Bear')

Philippe, Philippe Albert
Everyone knows his name

Toon Toon Toon

(To the tune of the Outhere Brothers, 'Boom Boom')

Toon, Toon, Toon, everybody say wheyaye (wheyaye)

Thank you very much

Thank you very much for the seven million
Thank you very much
Thank you very, very, very much
*(Sung to Man Utd, who included a struggling
striker in their line-up by the name of Andy Cole,
following his £7 million move from Newcastle)*

Sad Mackem Bastard

(to the tune of 'Daydream Believer')

Cheer up Peter Reid
Oh what can it mean
To a sad Mackem bastard
And a shit football team

Mackems on a string

(To the tune of 'My Ding-a-ling')

When I was a little bitty boy
My grandmother bought me a cute little toy
Two Sunderland fans, hanging on a string
She told me to kick their fucking heads in

Mackems on a string
Mackems on a string
She told me to kick their fucking heads in
Mackems on a string
Mackems on a string
She told me to kick their fucking heads in

Who's that team

Who's that team we call United
Who's that team we all adore
Oh, we play in black and white
And we all know how to fight
We'll support you ever more

NORWICH CITY

On the ball

On the ball City
Never mind the danger
Kick it off
Throw it in
Have a little scrimmage
Splendid rush
Bravo win or die
On the ball City
Never mind the danger

Iwan Roberts

Iwan, Iwan, Iwan
(Ironic attempt at encouraging Iwan Roberts)

NOTTINGHAM FOREST

City ground

(*To the tune of 'Mull of Kintyre'*)

Far have we travelled
And much have we seen
Goodison, Anfield are places we've been
Maine Road, Old Trafford still echo to the sounds
Of the boys in the Red shirts from City Ground
City Ground
Oh mist rolling in from the Trent
My desire is always to be there
On City Ground

Stevie Stone

Stevie Stone, Stevie Stone
Stevie, Stevie Stone
He's got no hair, but we don't care
Stevie, Stevie Stone

We hate Derby (1)

We hate Derby and we hate Derby
We hate Derby and we hate Derby
We are the Derby
Haters

Sheep shaggers

Sheep, sheep, sheep shaggers
Baaaaaaaaaaaaaa!!
(Well, if Derby will go and call themselves the Rams,
they can't expect much better)

We hate Derby (2)

Away in a manger
No crib for a bed
The little lord Jesus
Woke up and he said...
We hate Derby and we hate Derby
We hate Derby and we hate Derby
We are the Derby
Haters

Where's your caravan?
(To the tune of 'Where's Your Mama Gone?')

Where's your caravan, where's your caravan?
(Usually aimed at opposing players of 'gipsy' appearance)

Hello, hello

(To the tune of 'Marching through Georgia')

Hello, hello, we are the Trent End boys
Hello, hello you'll know us by our noise
We are the best team in the land
That no one can deny
We all follow the Forest

OLDHAM ATHLETIC

Come on, Oldham

Meat pie, sausage roll
Come on Oldham score a goal

PLYMOUTH ARGYLE

West Country

West Country, la la la
West Country, la la la

PORT VALE

The Wonder of you
(Another old chart-topper is resurrected)

Lou Macari

Lou, Lou, shit on the Lou
Lou, Lou, shit on the Lou
Lou, Lou, shit on the Lou
Shit on the Lou Macari
(Directed at former Stoke City manager Lou Macari)

Port Vale chant

Boing, boing, bag o' shit
(No love lost with West Brom)

Shittin' on the City

(To the tune of the 'Winter Wonderland')

Staffordshire
Are ya listening
To the song, we are singing
Walking along
Singing our songs
Shittin' on the City as we go

PRESTON NORTH END

Who's that jumping off the pier?

Who's that jumping off the pier?
Who's that jumping in the sea?
Oh it's Nigel and the boys
Making all the fucking noise
'Cos they can't beat the famous PNE

Sewing bags

He's sewing bags, he's sewing bags
He's sewing bags
Oyston's sewing bags
*(Reference to what the disgraced former Blackpool chairman
Owen Oyston now does with his time after being jailed)*

Preston chant

How wide do you want the goals?

QUEENS PARK RANGERS

2–1

2–1, you only beat us 2–1
When everyone else scores three,
You only beat us 2–1

*(Man City's anthem Blue Moon is thrown back at them after they
could only see off Rangers 2–1. The Londoners had suffered eight
straight defeats before this one)*

He's only a poor little Spurs fan

He's only a poor little Spurs fan
He stands at the back of the shelf
He goes to the bar
To buy a laaaaaa-ger
But only buys one for himself

Tony Adams

Who's that driving on the pavement
Who's that crashing through the wall
He plays in red and white
And he crashes every night
Tony Adams is a donkey after all

QPR chant

And its Queens Park Rangers
Queens Park Rangers FC
We're the finest football team
The world has ever seen

Steve Morrow

Morr-ow, Morrow fell off
Morr-ow, Morrow fell off
Morr-ow, Morrow fell off
Morrow fell off a donkey
(Skip to ma loo after Steve Morrow [who later moved to QPR]
jumped off Tony Adams's back in a game and broke his arm)

READING

We're Reading

We're Reading, we're Reading
We'll kick your fucking head in
(Aimed at a Cardiff City fan who climbed on to the
fence separating the two sets of fans during an
FA Cup tie at Elm Park in February 1998)

Reading chant

We support our local team
(Man Utd on the receiving end of this one
in FA Cup fourth round 1995–96)

ROCHDALE

Dale

Daaaaa-le
Daaaaa-le
Daaaaa-le

Robbie Painter

Super, super Rob
Super, super Rob
Super, super Rob
Super Robbie Painter

Johnnie Bowden

Na na na na, hey eeeeyyyy
Johnnie Bowden
*(His move to Oldham a few seasons ago cut Rochdale's
song output by a third, it would seem!)*

SCARBOROUGH

We're going up

We're going up, we're going up, we're going
Scarborough's going up

We hate City

We hate City, and we hate City
We hate City, and we hate City
We hate City, and we hate City
We are the City
Haters
(Neighbours and rivals York feel the force of this one)

Ben Worrall

He's small, he's bald
He's only three feet tall
Ben Worrall, Ben Worrall

Tom Mooney

Trifle, trifle, trifle
Let's have a Mooney rifle
(Encouragement for former favourite Tom Mooney)

SCUNTHORPE UNITED

Any old iron

Any old Iron, any old Iron, we sing, 'Up the Iron'
You look sweet, walking down the street
Bottle in ya hand and boots on yer feet
Dressed in style, nice big smile, we sing, 'Up the Iron'
And we don't give a damn for a Grimsby fan
Old Iron, old Iron

Scunthorpe

With an S and a C and a U N T
H and an O and an R P E
U-N-I-T-E-D
Scunthorpe United ... FC

We're Scunthorpe

Forever and ever
We follow our team
We're Scunthorpe United
We rule supreme
We'll never be mastered
By you Yorkshire bastards
We'll keep the Blue Flag flying high

SHEFFIELD UNITED

United chant

I was walking down Shoreham Street singing a song
Along came a pig fan and asked what's wrong
I kicked him in the balls and I kicked him in the head
Now that Wednesday fan is dead

The Grease Chip Buttie

You fill up my senses
Like a gallon of Magnet
Like a packet of Woodbines
Like a good pinch of snuff
Like a night out in Sheffield
Like a greasy chip buttie
Oh Sheffield United
Come thrill me again

SHEFFIELD WEDNESDAY

Wednesday chant

(*The* Great Escape *theme tune, accompanied*
by the splendid Hillsborough band)

Di Canio

D-I-CAN-IO

Singing the Blues

Never felt more like singing the Blues
Wednesday win, United lose
Oh Wednesday, you've got me singing the Blues

The Utrecht song

Daaa, da da da daaaa, dadadada, dadadada
dadadadaaaa
Da da daaaa, da da daa daaaa
Da da daa, da da da daaaa
WEDNESDAY!
(repeat ad infinitum)

(First appeared at the friendly against
FC Utrecht, Holland, summer 1996)

The Blue Flag

Forever and ever, we'll follow our team
Sheffield Wednesday, we are supreme
We'll never be mastered by no southern bastards
We'll keep the Blue Flag flying high

Sheffield Wednesday chant (1)

Sheeeee-field Wednesday
Hallelujah! Hallelujah!
(repeat)

Sheffield Wednesday chant (2)

There'll be a commotion when we win promotion
So score, Weeeddddd-nesday score

Emerson Thom

(To the tune of the 'Little Drummer Boy')

Soooo, they call him, Emerson Thom
A new-born king to us he's Emerson Thom
He looks like Paul Warhurst
He's Emerson Thom, Emerson Thom, Emerson Thom

Carlton Palmer/Nigel Jemson

We've got Carlton Palmer
He smokes marijuana
Ner ner, ner ner
Ner ner, ner ner

We've got Nigel Jemson
He smokes 20 Bensons
Ner ner, ner ner
Ner ner, ner ner

David Pleat

That's neat that's neat that's neat that's neat
We really love that David Pleat

Sheffield is wonderful

Oh Sheffield is wonderful
Oh Sheffield is wonderful
It's got tits, fanny and the Wednesday
Oh Sheffield is wonderful

SHREWSBURY TOWN

We all follow the Shrewsbury

We all follow the Shrewsbury
Over land and sea and WREXHAM!
We all follow the Shrewsbury
On to victory

Stevie Jagielka

La la la, la la la la, Stevie Jagielka
He's better than Brown, so come on Town
Telford United are going down
La la la, la la la la, Stevie Jagielka

My old man

My old man said follow the Town
And don't dilly dally on the way
We'll take the Station End and all that's in it
All get your boots on, we'll be there in a minute
With bottles and hammers, hatchets and spanners
We don't care what the fucking coppers say
'Cos we are the boys from the Gay, Gay Meadow

SOUTHAMPTON

When the Saints go marching in

Oh when the Saints
Go marching in
Oh when the Saints go marching in
I want to be in that number
Oh when the Saints go marching in
(in rounds)
Oh when the Saints (Oh when the Saints)
Go marching in (go marching in)

I comes down from Southampton

I can't read and I can't write
But that don't really matter
'Cos I comes down from Southampton
And I can drive a tractor

I can plough and milk a cow
And drive a great big mower
But the thing that I like best
Is being a strawberry grower
Oooooo-aaarrrrrrr
Oooooo-aaarrrrrrr
Ooooooo to be a Southernerrrrrrrrr

Alan Ball

He's short, he's fat
He's a ginger twat
Alan Ball, Alan Ball

Matt Le Tissier

Le Tiss, Le Tiss
Matt Matt Le Tiss
He gets the ball, he takes the piss
Matt Matt Le Tiss

SOUTHEND UNITED

Southend Pier

Oh Southend Pier
Is longer than yours
Oh Southend Pier is longer than yours
It's got some shops and a railway
Oh Southend Pier is longer than yours

*(Shrimpers supporters taunt fans of other teams based in seaside
resorts with this peculiar little number)*

STOKE CITY

Delilah

At the break of day when that man drove away
I was waiting, oh, oh, oh, oh
I crossed the street to her house
And she opened the door, oh, oh, oh, oh
She stood there laughing, ha, ha, ha, ha
I put my dick in her hand she laughed no more
Why why why Delilah
Why why why Delilah
So before they come to break down the door
Forgive me Delilah I just couldn't take any more

His name is Brian Little

His name is Brian Little
He's the boss of the team
He's the finest football manager
That the world has ever seen
We'll support him in the North stand
We're better than the Kop
If anybody comes up here
We'll kill the fucking lot

SUNDERLAND

Cheer up Peter Reid
(To the tune of 'Daydream Believer')

Oh I could fly without wings
On the back of Reidy's kings
At three o'clock I'm happy as can be
'Cos the good times they are here
And the Premiership is near
So watch out world as all of Roker sings

Chorus
Cheer up Peter Reid
Oh what can it mean
To a Sunderland supporter
To be top of the League

We once thought of you
As a Scouser dressed in blue
Now you're red and white through and through
We had all dreamt of the day
When a saviour would come our way
And now we know our dreams are coming true

I wish they all could be

(To the tune of 'California Girls')

Southwick girls are sexy
And the Hylton girls are hip
And the Farringdon girls are foxy
When they're giving you their lip

Downhill girls are daring
And the Tunstall girls are tops
And you can't go wrong
With Suzy Wong
And she comes from Marley Potts

Chorus
I wish they all could be from Sunderland
I wish they all could be from Sunderland
I wish they all could be Sunderland girls

I'm a believer (of Lee Clark)
(To the tune of 'I'm a Believer')

I thought class was only true in the Premier
Lee Lee Lee! Clark!
Meant for other fans, but not for us

Lee was ready for England
That's the way it seemed
One-touch football beating other teams

Chorus
Then I saw him play, now I'm a believer
Not a trace of mag in his genes
I'm in love, Ooooooooooh!
I'm a believer
I couldn't boo him if I tried

I thought goals were more or less never seen
Lee Lee Lee! Clark!
But the more he played the more we got. Oh yes!

What's the use in trying
All you get is pain
When you try to stop Clarkie playing his game

(Repeat chorus)

Fuck 'em all

Fuck 'em all, fuck 'em all
Dalglish McDermott and Hall
We'll never be mastered by black and white bastards
'Cos Sunderland's the best of them all

Top of the League
(To the tune of 'Top of the World')

We're on the
Top of the League looking
Down on the others
And the only explanation I can see
Is that one Peter Reid
Is all that we need
'Cos he took us to the top of the League

You sexy thing

I believe in miracles
Niall Quinn
You sexy thing

I believe in long balls
Since you came along, Niall Quinn

You're always injured Quinny
How did you know we'd put up with you?

How did you know we needed goals so badly?
How did you know, we'd sing for you gladly?

Yesterday, you were just a six-foot Irishman
Now you're putting headers away, scoring every match.

I believe in miracles
Niall Quinn
You sexy thing

I believe in long balls
Since you came along, Niall Quinn

You're always injured Quinny
But when you're not, you're our best hope

Yesterday, you were just a six-foot Irishman
Now you're putting headers away, scoring every match

I believe in miracles
Niall Quinn
You sexy thing

I believe in long balls
Since you came along, Niall Quinn

TORQUAY UNITED

Jack, Jack, Jack
(To the tune of 'Hot, Hot Hot')

O-way, O-way
O-way, O-way
Rodney Jack Jack Jack

One team in Devon

One team in Devon, there's only one team in Devon

I'm Torquay until I die

(To the tune of 'H.A.P.P.Y' theme of 1970s sitcom Only When I Laugh*)*

I'm Torquay 'til I die
I'm Torquay 'til I die
I know I am I'm sure I am
I'm Torquay 'til I die

TOTTENHAM HOTSPUR

Jürgen Klinsmann

He flies through the air with the greatest of ease
He never got touched, but he's down on his knees
(in honour of Jürgen Klinsmann)

Nayim

Nayim, from the halfway line
Nayim, from the halfway line
*(Ex-Spur who gunned down Arsenal with a spectacular goal
for Real Zaragoza in the dying seconds of the 1995 European
Cup-Winners' Cup Final)*

George Graham

Georgie Graham's magic
He wears a magic hat
And when he saw the agent's bung
He said I'm having that

He's only a poor little Gooner

He's only a poor little Gooner
He stands at the back of the Bank
He watches the reds, the football he dreads
So he ends up having a wank

He's only a poor little Gooner
His face is all tattered and torn
He made me feel sick, so I hit him with a brick
And now he don't sing anymore

Who's got a lovely wife?

Who's got a lovely wife?
Who's got a lovely wife?
Ian Walker, Ian Walker
He's got a lovely wife

Stand up if you hate stewards

Stand up if you hate stewards
Stand up if you hate stewards

You're not fit to wear the shirt

You'rrrreeee not fit to wear the shirt
You're not fit to wear the shirt

I wanna to be a scuba diver

I wanna be a scuba diver
And I wanna have a 69er
With the girl that I love the best
Many a night I sucked her breast
Fucked her standing
Fucked her flying
But now she's dead
But not forgotten
Dug her up and fucked her rotten

We hate Arsenal

We hate Arsenal and we hate Arsenal
We hate Arsenal and we hate Arsenal
We hate Arsenal and we hate Arsenal
We are the Arsenal
Haters

We are the Tottenham

We are the Tottenham, the pride of the South
We hate the Arsenal, 'cos they are all mouth
We took the North Bank, and that was fuck all
The Tottenham will rise and the Arsenal will fall

TRANMERE ROVERS

Oh Birkenhead

Oh Birkenhead
Is wonderful
Oh Birkenhead is won-der-ful
Full of tits and fannies and the Rovers
Oh Birkenhead is wonderful

We hate Scousers

We hate Scousers

We are not Scousers

Do not be mistaken, do not be misled
We are not Scousers, we're from Birkenhead
You can keep your cath-e-der-al
And Pier Head
We are not Scousers
We're from Birkenhead

WATFORD TOWN

Watford chant (1)
(To the tune of Cornershop's 'Brimful of Asha')

Give Lennie Lawrence his P-45

Watford chant (2)

Elton John's Taylor-made army

Stevie Palmer

There's only one Stevie Palmer
He smokes marijuana
Walking along, smoking a bong
Walking in a Palmer wonderland

WEST BROMWICH ALBION

WBA chant

Boing boing Baggies, boing boing

The Lord's my shepherd

The Lord's my shepherd
I'll not want
He makes me down to lie
In pastures green
He leadeth me
The quiet waters by

Stevie Bull's a Tatter

Stevie Bull's a tatter
He wears a tatter's hat
He plays for Wolverhampton
He's a fucking twat

He runs down the left wing
He runs down the right
He couldn't score a goal
If he played all fucking night

WEST HAM UNITED

Bernard Lama

We've got Bernard Lama
He smokes marijuana

She's a slag

She's a slag, and she's got no tits

You're shit

You're shit, and your bird's a slag

West Ham chant (1)

Does she take it up the arse?
*(Players with celebrity girlfriends come in for
special attention in these three chants)*

Ian Wright (1)
(Pre 1998–99 season)

Ian Wank, wank, wank
*(Former Arsenal striker Ian Wright always had a
habit of scoring against the Hammers)*

Ian Wright (2)
(1998–99 season onwards)

Ian Wright, Wright, Wright
(Following Wright's signing for the Hammers from Arsenal)

West Ham chant (2)

1–0 to the Cockney boys
1–0 to the Cockney boys

WIGAN ATHLETIC

You can stick yer fucking rugby up yer arse

You can stick yer fucking rugby up yer arse
You can stick yer fucking rugby up yer arse
You can stick yer fucking rugby
You can stick yer fucking rugby
Stick yer fucking rugby up yer arse
*(Bodes well for the imminent ground-sharing
arrangements with Wigan Rugby League Club)*

Merry Christmas

So here it is
Merry Christmas
Everybody's having fun
Bollocks to you Preston cunts
We've beaten you 2–1
*(Slade's Christmas party anthem is used to spread
a little seasonal cheer among Wigan's rivals)*

Build a bonfire

(To the tune of 'My Darling Clementine')

Build a bonfire, build a bonfire
Stick Preston on the top
Put Burnley in the middle
And burn the fucking lot

You are my sunshine

(All together now)
You are my sunshine, my only sunshine
You make me happy, when skies are blue
I never notice, how much I miss you
Until they take my sunshine away

WIMBLEDON

We are the Wombles

We won't win the League and we won't win the Cup
We're not going down and we're not going up
We're not very good in fact we're bad
We are the Wombles, we're mad

Winter holiday
(To the tune of 'Summer Holiday')

Palace are going on a winter holiday
They are going for a season or two
They are going to a place called the Nationwide
That's the place for yooooooouuuu
For a season or two

Palace go down
(To the tune of 'Tupthumping' by Chumbawumba)

Palace go down
They come back up again
But then they always go back down

Palace go down
They come back up again
But then they always go back down

We hate the Palace scum
We hate the Palace scum

They're just a shitty team
They're just a crappy team
They're just a bollocks team
They're just a wanky team

They're just a team that reminds us of a bag of shit
They're just a team that reminds us of a sack of shit

Oh, Palace scum
Palace scum
Palace scum

Palace go down

The Dons belong in Merton

(To the tune of Oasis's 'Dont look back in anger')

Look inside the eye of Sam's mind
Talking from his behind
About a place to play

We know just where he has been
It's only Dublin he's seen
It gives the game away

But to find a ground in Merton can't be hard
All this council stuff could be just a charade
And millionaires that we have never seen
Have walked right in and they have hid
Behind their 30 million quid
But they ain't ever gonna wipe our club out

And no Sam we can't wait
To walk through the gates
Of a new ground back home
You'll listen one day
The Dons belong in Merton
You'll hear us say

WYCOMBE WANDERERS

A decent referee
(To the tune of 'Yellow Submarine')

All we want is a decent referee
A decent referee, a decent referee

Kavanagh

Oooo-aaaa
Kavanagh

YORK CITY

Andy Mac

Oh Andy Mac is our full back
Oh Andy Mac is our full back
(Andy McMillan earns the plaudits)

Rodney Rowe

Rodney Rowe, Rowe, Rowe
Rodney Rowe, Rowe, Rowe
(The next Ian Wright then, lads!)

York chant (1)

Three-nil, we beat Man U three-nil

York chant (2)

Are you Scarborough in disguise?

York chant (3)

What's it like to be outclassed?
(Three classics born out of the Coca-Cup
triumph over Alex Ferguson's troops)

York chant (4)

Red army, red army, red army

You're going in the Ouse

You're going in the Ouse, you're going in the Ouse
And now you're gonna believe us
And now you're gonna believe us
You're going in the Ouse
(The Minstermen's faithful offer visitors an unexpected
chance to sample the delights of the city's river)

Y-R-A

Y-R-A, we're Yorkshire's Republican Army
We're barmy wherever we go
We fight friend and foe
'Cos we are the Y-R-A

The pride of all Yorkshire

We are the pride of all Yorkshire, the Cock of the North
We hate Leeds United and Scarborough of course
We kick in the 'Boro until they go down
'Cos the City boys are in town

Third Division rubbish

Third Division rubbish, you're Third Division rubbish

We're North Yorkshire's only one

North Yorkshire's only one
North Yorkshire's only one
And are you going to believe us
We're North Yorkshire's only one

General Songs

Variations of these songs can be heard at many grounds throughout the country

Wonderland

One Dennis Bergkamp
There's only one Dennis Bergkamp
Walking along, singing a song
Walking in a Bergkamp wonderland

Super Nick

Super super Nick
Super super Nick
Super super Nick
Super Nick Anelka

One Michael Owen

One Michael Owen
There's only one Michael Owen
One Michael Owen
There's only one Michael Owen

Teddy Sheringham

Oh Teddy Teddy
Teddy Teddy Teddy Teddy Sheringham

You are my sunshine

You are my Villa, my only Villa,
You make me happy, when skies are grey
I never notice how much I love you
Until they take my Villa away

Dublin's fair city

In Dublin's fair city
Where the girls are so pretty
I first set my eyes on sweet Molly Malone
Through streets broad and narrow
She wheeled her wheelbarrow
Singing ... Bournemouth

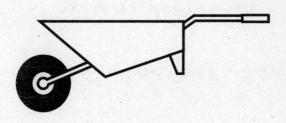

The Greatest
(To the tune of 'The Wild Rover')

And it's Aston Villa
Aston Villa FC
We're by far the greatest team
The world has ever seen

Lucky Arsenal

Lucky, lucky Arsenal!

Can we play you every week

Can we play you
Can we play you
Can we play you every week?

Can you hear?

Can you here the Shitty Sing?
No-oh
No-oh
Can you here the Shitty Sing?
No-oh
No-oh
Can you hear the Shitty sing?
'Cos I can't hear a fucking thing
Oh-oh the Shitty!
Ahhhhhhhhhhhhhhhhh!
(Used for any team who include City in their name)

Referee songs
(1)
The referee's a wanker

(2)
Who's the bastard in the black

(3)
Who's the bastard in the green
(Introduced when the referees' shirts changed)

Jingle Bells

Jingle Bells, Jingle Bells
Jingle all the way,
Oh what fun it is to sing
When the Wanderers win away

We shall not be moved

We shall not
We shall not be moved
We shall not
We shall not be moved
We've got the team, the score
to win the Football League*
We shall not be moved

*can be 'FA Cup'

The Famous

The famous Man United went to Rome to see the Pope
The famous Man United went to Rome to see the Pope
The famous Man United went to Rome to see the Pope
And this is what he said: 'Fuck Off'
Who the fuck are Man United
Who the fuck are Man United
Who the fuck are Man United
When the whites go marching on, on, on

We had joy

We had joy, we had fun
We had Arsenal on the run
But the joy couldn't last
'Cos the bastards ran too fast

Score in a brothel

Score in a brothel
You couldn't score in a brothel

Who ate all the pies

Who ate all the pies?
Who ate all the pies?
You fat bastard, you fat bastard
You ate all the pies

Let him die

Let him die, let him die, let him die
(Sympathy for the injured opposing player)

You're gonna get...

You're gonna get your fuckin' heads kicked in

You're so shit

You're so shit it's unbelievable

Let's all have a disco

Let's all have a disco
Lets's all have a disco
La, la, la, la, Oi
La, la, la, la, Oi

Que sera

Que sera, sera
Whatever will be, will be
We're going to Wem-ber-ley
Que sera, sera

What's the score?

Seaman, what's the score
Seaman, Seaman, what's the score

Generally directed at your goalie (if you're winning)

We will follow

We will follow the Bolton
Over land and sea (and Blackpool)
We will follow the Bolton
On to viiiiic-to-ry

England
Team
Songs

No surrender

Give me St George in my heart, keep me English
Give me St George in my heart, I say
Give me St George in my heart, keep me English
Keep me English to my dying day
No surrender
No surrender
No surrender to the IRA (scum)

England chant

Inger-land, Inger-land, Inger-land
Inger-land, Inger-land, Inger-land
Inger-land, Inger-land, Inger-land
Inger-land
INGER-LAND
(Repeat for most of the match)

The Great Escape

Da-da, da-da da

Da-da, da-da da

Da-da, da-da da-da da-darrr

ENGLAND

(Repeat for most of the match)

Rule Britannia

Rule Britannia
Britannia rules the waves
Britains never never never shall be slaves

If it wasn't for...

If it wasn't for the English you'd be Krauts
If it wasn't for the English you'd be Krauts
If it wasn't for the English
Wasn't for the English
If it wasn't for the English you'd be Krauts
(To be sung in France)

Two World Wars

Two World Wars and one World Cup
Doo dar, doo dar
Two World Wars and one World Cup
Doo dar, doo dar day
(To be sung whenever Germans are near)

Scottish football Clubs

DUNDEE

The James Grady Macarena

He's five foot two and his name is Jamesie Grady
He gets the ball and he goes off on a mazy
He's from Clydebank and he's pure fuckin' crazy
Oh Jamesie Grady

Top of the League

You know, you know
We're top of the League and you're no'
You know, you know
We're top of the League and you're no'
Top of the League, oh yes we're top of the League
We're top of the League and you're no'

As I was walking

As I was walking down the Overgate
I met wee Tommy Scobie
And he said to me
'Would you like to see the famous Dundee FC?'

So we went along to Dens Park
To see the famous XI
But when we got there
The terracing was bare
And we'd gave United seven

DUNDEE UNITED

The Dens Park Massacre of '65

Get down on your knees and pray
It's the anniversary
Of the Dens Park massacre of '65 (65!)
It's the day we won't forget
And the Dundee will regret
It's the day we gave them 1-2-3-4-5!

It was the 11th of September
A day we all remember
Finn Dossing was at centre and scored three
Lennart Wing from the spot
And Gillespie with a shot
A shot that Ally Packy didn't see

United boys

Hello! Hello! We are United boys
Hello! Hello! You'll tell us by our noise
We're up to our knees in Derry boys
Surrender or you'll die
For we are United boys

Let's all laugh at Dundee

Let's all laugh at Dundee
Haha ha ha, haha ha ha

HEARTS

I was born under an orange scarf
(To the tune of the 'I was born under a Wandering Star')

I was born under an orange scarf
I was born under an orange scarf
Do you know where hell is?
Hell is Easter Road
Heaven is Tynecastle
Where the Fenians crap their load
Oh, I was born under an orange scarf

We're going to Europe
(To the tune of the 'My Way')

And now, the end is near
We've followed Hearts, from Perth to Paisley
We've travelled far, by bus and car
And other times, we've went by railway
We've been, to Aberdeen
We hate the Hibs, they make us spew up
So make a noise you Gorgie Boys
We're going to Europe

To see, HMFC
We'll even dig, the Channel Tunnel
When we're afloat, on some big boat
We'll tie our scarves, around the funnel
We have no cares, for other players
Like Rossi, Boniek or Tardelli
When we're overseas, the Hibs will be
In Portobelly
The might of Europe

We all can laugh, at Hibs
When we play Chelsea, Metz or Inter
They'll be up at Dundee
And relegated by mid-winter
While we go, marching on
And show the Huns, the way to do it
They lost again, while we had slain
The might of Europe

The day's, not far away
When we will reach, the heights of glory
We'll follow Hearts, through foreign parts
And Gorgie Boys, will tell the story
How we scored three, at Napoli
Hibs lost away, again, at Greenock
When Hibs went down, we took the crown
As Kings of Europe

H-E-A-R-T-S

Away up in Gorgie at Tynecastle Park
There's a wee fitba' team that will aye make its mark
They've won all the honours in footballing arts
And there's nae ither team to compare with the Hearts

Chorus
H-E-A-R-T-S
If you cannae spell it then here's what it says
Hearts, Hearts, glorious Hearts
It's down at Tynecastle they bide
The talk of the toon are the boys in maroon
And Auld Reekie supports them with pride

This is my story, this is my song
Follow the Hearts and you can't go wrong
Oh some say that Celtic and Rangers are grand
But the boys in maroon are the best in the land

We've won the League flag and we've won the
League Cup
Though we sometimes go down we can aye go back up
Our forwards can score and it's no idle talk
Our defence is as strong as the auld castle rock

National caps we can always supply
Like Massey and Walker and Bauld and Mackay
If I had the time I could name dozens more
Who've helped in producing the auld Hampden roar

CELTIC

The Celtic Song

Hail, Hail, the Celts are here
What the hell do we care
What the hell do we care
Hail, Hail, the Celts are here
What the hell do we care now...

For it's a grand old team to play for
For it's a grand old team to see
And if you know the history
It's enough to make your heart go
Nine-in-a-row

We don't care what the animals say
What the hell do we care
For all we know
Is that there's going to be a show
And that Glasgow Celtic will be there

The Coronation Cup

Said Lizzie to Philip as they sat down to dine
I've just had a note from a good friend of mine
His name is big Geordie, he's loyal and true
And his big dirty nose is a bright shade of blue

He says that the Rangers are right on their game
And he asks for a trophy to add to their fame
We'll send them a trophy that the Rangers can win
Said Philip to Lizzie, 'Watch the Celts don't step in'

Said Lizzie to Philip they don't stand a chance
I'll send up my Gunners to lead them a dance
With the Celtic defeated, the way will be clear
And a trophy for the Rangers in my crowning year

Alas, and alas, for the wearers of blue
The Celts beat the Arsenal and the Manchester too
Beat Hibs in the final, and lo and behold
All of Hampden was covered in green, white and gold

Said Lizzie to Philip when she heard the news
So tell me dear Philip, for you ought to know
How to beat Glasgow Celtic and keep them below

Said Philip to Lizzie, there's only one way
And I've known the secret for many a day
To beat Glasgow Celtic, you'll have to deport
All the fighting mad Irish that give them support

The Fields of Athenry

By a lonely prison wall, I heard a young girl calling
Michael they have taken you away
For you stole Travelyan's corn, so the young might see
the morn
Now a prison ship lies waiting in the bay

Chorus
Low lie the Fields of Athenry
Where once we watched the small, free birds fly
Our love was on the wing, we had dreams and songs to
sing
It's so lonely on the Fields of Athenry

By a lonely prison wall, I heard the young man calling
Nothing matters Mary when you are free
'Gainst the famine and the crown, I rebelled they cut
me down
Now you must raise our child in dignity

Chorus
By a lonely harbour wall, she watched the last star
falling
As the prison ship sailed out against the sky
Now she'll wait and hope and pray, for her love in
Botany Bay
It's so lonely round the Fields of Athenry

Celtic is the name

In Glasgow town we have a team and Celtic is the name
We've beaten Rangers and Milan for Celtic know the game
And if you don't believe me boys then come and see us
play
For Glasgow Celtic, up the Celtic, beats the world today
For Glasgow Celtic, up the Celtic, beats the world today

We are a famous football team I'm sure you all agree
We've played them all, the big and small, from Lisbon
to Dundee
And if you don't believe me, boys, then this to you I say
Come up the Parkhead, dear old Parkhead, Celtic leads
the way
Come up the Parkhead, dear old Parkhead, Celtic leads
the way

In Glasgow town we have a team and Celtic is the name
We've beaten Rangers and Milan for Celtic know the game
And if you don't believe me boys then come and see us
play
For Glasgow Celtic, up the Celtic, beats the world today
For Glasgow Celtic, up the Celtic, beats the world today

The flags are out for Celtic

The flags are gaily flying o'er Celtic Park today
Because the lads of Celtic have shown the world the way
They played the game in Lisbon and here is how they won
They didn't play defensive, attack is what they done

The flags are out for Celtic, they know just what to do
And Scottish hearts and Irish hearts are
mighty proud of you

In all the big world over the name of Celtic rung
And in our heart of Glasgow our Celtic song was sung
God bless you great XI, this is our greatest day
Next season Jock from Greenock we're with
you all the way

The flags are out for Celtic, they know just what to do
And Scottish hearts and Irish hearts are
mighty proud of you

You won so many cups this year, four or five or six
You should give one to Rangers, they're really in a fix
John Lawrence shook your hands lads as
you came off the plane
And everyone is proud of you, your football brought
you fame

The flags are out for Celtic, they know just what to do
And Scottish hearts and Irish hearts are
mighty proud of you

PARTICK THISTLE

Mary from Maryhill

I love a lassie
A bonny bonny lassie
She's as thin as the paper on the wall
Legs like a spider
I'd like to fuckin' ride her
Mary from Maryhill

RANGERS

The Sash

For it's here I am an Orangeman, just come across the sea
For singing and for dancing, I hope that I'll please thee
I can sing and dance with any man, as I did in days of yore
And its on the twelfth I long to wear the sash
my father wore

It is old but it is beautiful and it's colours they are fine
It was worn at Derry, Aughrim, Enniskillen and the Boyne
My Father wore it as a youth in bygone days of yore
And its on the twelfth I long to wear, the sash
my father wore

For it's now I'm going to leave you, good luck to
you I'll say
And when I'm on the ocean deep, I hope for me
you'll pray
I'm going to my native land, to a place they call Dromore,
Where on the twelfth I long to wear the sash
my father wore

Whenever I come back again my brethren here to see
I hope to find old Orange style, they will always
welcome me
My favourite tune's 'Boyne Water', but to please
me more and more,
And make my Orange heart full glad with the
Sash my Father wore

211

The Sash (2)

It is old but it is beautiful, it's red, it's white and it's blue
It's worn on the slopes of Ibrox Park, and a place called
Parkhead too
My father wore it as a youth in the bygone days of yore
And it's on display every Saturday
Every time the Rangers score

The Famous royal blue

For ever and ever, we'll follow the Gers
The Glasgow Rangers, the Teddy Bears
For we will be mastered, by whom, by no Fenian bastards
We'll keep the Blue Flag flying high

Soooooo, bring on the Hibs, the Hearts, the Celtic
Bring on the Spaniards by the score
Barcelona, Real Madrid
Who the hell are you trying to kid
For we're out to show the world what we can do

I have often heard that Real Madrid is the greatest
football team
I have even heard that Anderlecht, is the best you
have ever seen
There's Manchester United, and there's
Tottenham Hotspur, too
There is Everton, Burnley, Blackburn, just to
name a famous few

Who's that team we call the Rangers
Who's that team we all adore
They're the boys in royal blue and they are
Scotland's gallant few
And we are out to show the world what we can do

So bring on the Hibs, the Hearts, the Celtic
Bring on Spaniards by the score
And we will hope that every game, we will imortalise
the name
Of the boys that wear the famous royal blue

The Billy Boys

Hello, hello, we are the Billy Boys
Hello, hello, you'll know us by our noise
We're up to our necks in Fenian blood
Surrender or you'll die
'Cos we are the Bridgestown Boys

Scotland Team Songs

Ally's Army

We're on the drugs with Ally's Army
We're all taking Benzadrine
And we'll really shake them up
When we drink it out of a cup
'Cos Scotland are the greatest football team

William Wallace

Scots, wha hae wi' Wallace bled
Scots, wham Bruce has aften led
Welcome to your gory bed
Or to victory

Loch Lomond

By yon bonnie bank and by yon bonnie braes
Where the sun shines bright on Loch Lomond
Where me and my true love were ever wont to gae
On the bonnie, bonnie banks of Loch Lomond

For you'll take the high road and I'll take the low road
And I'll be in Scotland afore ye
Where me and my true love will never meet again
By the bonnie, bonnnie banks of Loch Lomond

Hokey Cokey

You put your left hand in
You take your left hand out
You put your left hand in and you shake it all about
You do the hokey cokey and you turn around
That's what it's all about
Oh Diego Maradona
Oh Diego Maradona
Oh Diego Maradona
He put the English out, out, out

Where's yir father?

Where's yir father
Where's yir father
Where's yir father, referee?

Yi havna got one
Yi havna got one
Yir a bastard referee

Famous Tartan Army

We're the famous Tartan Army and we're off to gay
Paree
Gay Paree
Gay Paree
We're the famous Tartan Army and we're off to gay
Paree

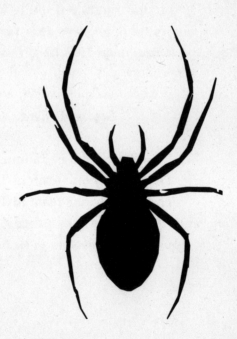

Stand up

Stand up if you hate England
(etc.)

Sing when you're whaling

Sing when you're whaling
You only sing when you're whaling
*(Sung by the Tartan Army when Scotland played
Norway in the 1998 World Cup finals)*

Scotland chant

One team in Tallinn
There's only one team in Tallinn
There's only one team in Tallinn
*(Sung by the Tartan Army when Estonia failed to turn up for
their 1996 World Cup qualifier in the Estonian capital)*

Everywhere we go

Everywhere we go
People want to know
Who we are
So we're gonna tell them
We're mental and we're barmy
We're the famous Tartan Army
Ooooooooh
Ooooooooh
Oooooh Scotland
Scotland
I'd walk a million miles
For one of your goals
Oh Scotland

ACKNOWLEDGEMENTS

Many thanks to all the football clubs, their fanzines and supporters whose help was invaluable in producing this compilation.

Special thanks to the following:
Two Together, Barnet fanzine; Mick Gething and Ruth Huggett, Bolton Wanderers Supporters Club (London); *The City Gent*, Bradford City fanzine; Andrew Turton at *The Thin Blue Line*, Cardiff City fanzine; Les Motherby at *Amber Nectar*, Hull City fanzine; John 'Marching On Together' Hughes, Leeds United fanatic; *Dante Friend*, The Independent Manchester City Fans' Line; *Fly Me To The Moon*, Middlesbrough fanzine; Simon Sephton, Scunthorpe United programme editor; Rob Offer's *Stadium of Light* website and Kev Howard for their Sunderland input; Gavin Mortimer, Tartan Army foot soldier; John 'The Baggie' Owen, WBA fanatic; Xavier Wiggins at *Hoof The Ball Up*, Wimbledon fanzine. Apologies to anyone I've not mentioned.